Inspired Madness

J.POPE ©

Inspired Madness

The Gifts of Burning Man

Dale Pendell

Frog, Ltd.
Berkeley, California

Published by Frog, Ltd.

Frog, Ltd. books are distributed by
North Atlantic Books
P.O. Box 12327
Berkeley, California 94712

Cover art by Dale Pendell
Illustrations reproduced by permission of Mira Talbott-Pope.
Cover design and book design by Brad Greene
Printed in the United States of America

North Atlantic Books' publications are available through most bookstores. For further information, call 800-337-2665 or visit our website at www.northatlanticbooks.com.

Substantial discounts on bulk quantities are available to corporations, professional associations, and other organizations. For details and discount information, contact our special sales department.

Library of Congress Cataloging-in-Publication Data

Pendell, Dale, 1947–
    Inspired madness : the gifts of Burning Man / Dale Pendell.
       p. cm.
    ISBN-13: 978-1-58394-172-0 (pbk.)
    ISBN-10: 1-58394-172-X (pbk.)
    1. Burning Man (Festival) 2. Performance art—Nevada—Black Rock Desert.
3. Counterculture—Nevada—Black Rock Desert. I. Title.
    NX510.N32B637 2006
    394.2509793'54—dc22
                                                            2006024549
                                                            CIP

1 2 3 4 5 6 7 8 9 UNITED 12 11 10 09 08 07 06

For Laura and her fine ear;
for Benny and The Fun House Family,
who first invited me to the Playa;
and to all those who create beauty in the spirit of giving.

 or nearly twenty years thousands of artists, dancers, visionaries, and misfits have converged on Nevada's Black Rock Desert at the end of August to create an electrified city on an ancient lake bed called the Playa. A week later it all disappears. It could be called Art, a Happening, a Festival, a Social Experiment, a Potlatch, or all of the above. It's Burning Man. No single account can come close to being an adequate description. This (unauthorized, unofficial, and sometimes irreverent)

account seeks to examine a few of Burning Man's many manifestations. The book is loosely arranged into three interleaved sections called "On the Playa" (vignettes), "Burning Man" (history), and "Potlatch" (theory). Veteran Burners will recognize that while some of the events described are from 2004, some are from earlier years. Some are from more recent years. The mixing is promiscuous. Some of the events are only remembered by the author, and may have been hallucinations.

Dust Devils

They came from the dust and spread nylon wings where the great fish died, sun-flopping whiffs on crumbling parchment in a dried bottle, purpled to whom it may concern: bone dust, infused smoke, forgot that, ice sheets, once.

They arose flapping, mud-cracked swarms, a gun to their heads, Caesar's shadow, rusted nails of the time when there were ships and curled horns and ivory pendants, clay-eaters from fracture in silica, long pennants of wind song converging on the ash-rising flames. New top-hats of a dry resurrection, thorn-born and thyrsus-armed in the final days, snakes awoken by din of feathers and the shattering of pots, shadow cleft beneath jack boot, boulevards seeking the shade of a Babylonian willow, chrysalis of locust, eyeglass of dried scales, sandals following a whirlwind of fire, iron tools and tambourines while the old blood burns, Croesus' gold at the oracle's camel-boned feet.

They emerged from cracked sidewalks, ghostly and blaring an earthquake dream, cracked feet to crack an anesthetized fault, scorpions wriggling: the women bared their breasts, worm twitch at the end of an age. They rose from graves, erosion-breached, poked and stuck, syringe derrick, beached tankers amid the campfires, black smoke, panther shadows, flickers in Old Town, six-legged scuttle in a carbonate sink, coffee cup crust rattling "Adonai, Adonai" in a new tectonic fold.

They appeared like gypsum, oil-skinned in the naked sand, sabers in a pile, hoof beats of a gunpowder séance tomb-lit by nitrate tallow. Detritis, curb-nurtured babble rebuilding the Tower from impatient dust.

On the Playa

As you arrive on the Playa, after your long drive through the spectacular desert of the Great Basin, after passing beautiful Pyramid Lake and miles and miles of sagebrush, and after waiting your turn in the line of already dusty cars, you come to the Greeters. Our Greeter was named SandKiss. She was wearing a net top. There were other Greeters who were completely naked, but there is something about net tops—I couldn't take my eyes off her breasts. She took a step closer so that her breasts filled the window, which was open.

"Is that OK?"

"Yes," I said.

What had I agreed to? She'd just asked me a series of questions. It could have been anything: maybe it was "Now we're going to take your shoes away from you" or "You may be sacrificed."

"Yes," I repeated, "absolutely."

And we drove through. With a wonderful map showing the location of more than four hundred and fifty registered "theme camps," and a forty-page booklet listing the week's special events.

I scanned the pamphlet. There were 12-Step meetings at Anonymous Camp. There were scores of workshops and classes, from

turban wrapping to foot care; fire dancing and pole dancing;
yoga and tantric sex; African drumming and Israeli dancing;
massage, hypnosis, "used eyeglass recycling," tooth flossing,
joke telling, and eye gazing. And in addition to the classes and
workshops there were at least eight hundred other "events."

Roving Whores Camp:
"Each night TempleWhore will send out roving whores to another
camp to descend on a chosen few, offering to these select the true
keys to the vault of heaven."

"The Vault of Heaven" was this year's theme.

Camp Everyone—Threesome Thursday:
"Ah, the big challenge. Who will join
you? Will it be a him or a her? Or both?
Go out on a limb and invite another to
join you. . . ."

Pandora's Matchbox Cocktail Lounge &
Space Station: Ass-Less Chaps Social
Hour & Fashion Show.

There was "fine dining at Chez Snug-
gle and Pink Tantric Puja," the "Naked
Psychedelic Ritual Dance," the "French
Maid Brigade Parade," hosted by Le

Consulat General de France (a Black Rock City Sunset Samba Circus), the "Black Rock City Int'l Kite Festival," hosted by the Black Rock City Department of Tethered Aviation, and "Brainwave Scans" at Automatic Unconscious. Orgasmateria, part of Asylum, was advertising a "Carpet-Munching Workshop":

> *"This is a hands-on interactive event. Bring your own carpet, hardwood floor is welcome. Single carpets will be accommodated. Please properly shampoo the rug, or mop the floor before coming. This is not a spectator event, bring no cameras."*

Burning Man again. I was home. And Burning Man wasn't even here yet. One could see a handful of camps clustered across the alkali flats, and the construction on Center Camp was moving along, but mostly it was still empty desert, it was "playa"—an ancient lake bed composed of clay, carbonates, alkali, gypsum, and thousands or millions of tons of the finest and roundest dust particles to be found anywhere in the world. Some say the Black Rock Desert is the largest expanse of absolutely flat ground anywhere in the United States, though I've heard the same thing about the Bonneville Salt Flats.

Surveyor flags marked out the roads and the lot divisions for the inner camps. It was Saturday and we were the first kids on the block. Owl arced out the circle of the dome with a surveyor's tape. We stared at the ground and paced around, talking about how to arrange the camp. Finally we were able to throw tarps down on a spot that was *not* going to be a campsite, and to unload all the trucks into a huge pile of tools, gear, building materials, boxes, tents, bicycles, food, gasoline, water, speakers, and musical apparatus that would constitute our material possessions for the next week and a half—everything that a camp of twenty might need to survive and prosper on an alkali flat well-known for some of the harshest and most extreme weather in the West.

Burning Man

Black Rock City is laid out on polar coordinates. The radial spokes are named by hour and half-hour: "6:30," "3:00." The names of the concentric circles vary year to year with the theme. In 2004, with its "Vault of Heaven" theme, the circles were named for the planets, the innermost circle, as always, just called "the Esplanade," and the outermost circle, in this case beyond Pluto, called "Sedna."

The "registered" camps are placed in the two innermost blocks of the City's great circles. Beyond them, in the outer circles, are hundreds of other "unregistered" theme camps, and the thousands of other camps, individual or collective, that constitute Black Rock City. Sometimes a camp is just an RV, parked somewhere around 9:30 and Neptune. Or a trailer, or a few tents. But the more typical camp is a group of friends, with individual tents or sleeping alcoves built around a central shade structure. The materials and engineering of shade structures is a study in itself: some are domes, others elaborate variations of PVC and tarps. Some use wood, some use metal electrical conduit. Some of the materials are difficult to identify. Nothing can be flimsy, however. Everything has to be able to weather the ferocious windstorms that are common on the Black Rock.

Some camps are huge, occupying an entire block and composed of hundreds of people. Sometimes they are loose collectives based on geography, such as Mystic Beat, a group from Sonoma County, California. Others are more tightly knit tribes that have been together for years. Others are "villages," groups of smaller camps that have gotten together to share a basic infrastructure. One camp that placed themselves on the outskirts pulled together RVs bumper to bumper all around their camp to close it in. They had a swimming pool.

Mystic Beat Lounge
Otter Camp
Critical Tits Camp
T.A.Z.
Hushville
Brane

Penetration Village / Jiffy Lube
Gigsville
Woonami
Asylum

On the Playa

Jah and Snooker didn't arrive until well after midnight, but they decided that they'd rather set up in the dark than in the heat. There was half a moon and some reflected glow from Roller Disco, setting up with a noisy generator and arc-lamps across the street. Jah and Snooker put up a long hogan, about twelve by forty, and pitched their individual tents inside of that.

Burning Man

What is Burning Man? Well, it *so* depends on who's asking. For some of the people in America, it's best that they never know or hear of it. If they really knew, there's nothing they wouldn't stoop to in their effort to stop it.

Yeah, the next thing you know there'd be undercover agents on the Playa.

If you are talking to a potential date for next year's burn, you can say, "It's an orgy of sex and drugs." If you're talking to your mother, you say, "Oh, it's ... kind of an arts festival, Mom." If you're talking to brainy radical types, you mumble something about "anarchism" or "an experiment in alternative social organization."

Trying to tell what Burning Man is like to someone who has never been there inevitably brings up some version of "It's like trying to explain [sex, color, New York City, LSD, etc., etc.] to [a virgin, the blind from birth, an alien from Alpha Centauri, etc. etc.]. The opening line on the Burning Man website uses the "color/blind" variation. But how many times do you want to hear "You have to be there"? Well, one more time. It's true. If there is one constant among newbies (those attending for the first time), it is "*Nothing* could have prepared me for *this*."

All of this "Wow!" is very annoying to people who haven't been and don't particularly want to go to Burning Man. "Can't describe it," they will mock, "what kind of a writer are you? *We* describe the ineffable experience of Art and Theater every week in our columns." Which is true enough, more enough sometimes than others, but for the most part the critics speak as spectators, which for Burning Man is *not* the experience.

And then there is the matter of scale.

Yes. And the matter of dust.

One friend who came to Burning Man for the first time described it as a cross between a Fellini movie and Mad Max.

I would throw in "Wicker Man" and John Waters. Most of all it's a potlatch, a crazed Dionysian festival complete with dismemberment, where the art is in giving.

Potlatch

Potlatch, from a Nootka word meaning "gift" or "giving," was the ceremonial festival of Native Americans of the Northwest Coast characterized by ostentatious gift-giving and the lavish destruction of personal property, thus emphasizing the social prestige of the host. Marcel Mauss used the potlatch as a key to understanding the archaic gift-economy that sustained early human social organization. His ideas have been elaborated and extended by Claude Lévi-Strauss, Marshall Sahlins *(Stone Age Economics)*, Lewis Hyde *(The Gift)*, Georges Bataille *(The Accursed Share)*, and Norman O. Brown. Brown was most influenced by Bataille, and he considers Hyde's account to have understated the dark and self-destructive side of potlatch. Brown's ideas are contained in his last published essay, a remarkable piece called "Dionysus in 1990," included in *Apocalypse And/Or Metamorphosis.*

> The key move in Bataille's transvaluation of economic value is to deflect the traditional Marxist notion of a "surplus" by connecting it with the Dionysian notion of life as the manifestation of a universal principle of excess.

The whole notion of "surplus" then begins to waver: if there is no distinction between necessary and wasteful expenditure, if there is a necessity to waste, where is the "surplus"? The focus shifts from modes of production to modes of unproductive expenditure; from production to consumption; unnecessary, unconditional, exuberant, i.e., wasteful consumption. (Brown 1991, p. 185)

The idea of "wasteful consumption" is anathema to both conservationists of the old school and their more radical brethren, the Deep Ecologists, as well as to main-line Protestants—even if they drive SUVs. It's probably anathema to just about everyone. It is, frankly, madness. Brown bets all with Socrates, in *Phaedrus*, that if the madness is divine madness, that is, the gift of a god (such as Dionysus), it is the source of our greatest blessings. This is of course a wager. We can't prove it.

Madness is inherent in life and in order to live with it we must learn to love it. This is the point of honoring it with the name of a god. (Brown 1991, p. 180)

Burning Man

For radical eco-philes, there is plenty about Burning Man not to like—it's techno, it's fossil fuel-intensive, it's almost wholly driven by canned music, and it more and more resembles a freaky version of the Vegas strip than an art happening. Sense of place, aside from the laudable "leave no trace" ethic, is, with a few (striking) exceptions, more absent than present.

Suzanne was annoyed by "the little boy energy"—let's make a bang, let's blow it up, let's make a bigger flash.

With so much "not to like," why do so many of us become confirmed "Burners," to whom the "Welcome Home" of the Greeters is not the least bit ironic? Maybe the "not to like" is a filter—it keeps away our more judgmental friends, those who would find too much fault and thereby inhibit us.

The "little boy energy" didn't bother me much—I'm kinda that way myself—though I do prefer the fire spinners and the poi twirlers to the giant propane cannons mounted on flatbeds which always seem a little like self-propelled-howitzer wannabes. The Mad Max side lacks the *inner* fire of the psychedelic fun houses, but, well, that's just me, folks.

And "Leave No Trace" should not be dismissed as mere cute slogan. It is the single most radical and revolutionary ethic of Burning Man, even more far-reaching than the absence of corporate commerce. After Burning Man, slag heaps, stumped mountainsides, poisoned rivers, and polluted air are as ugly ethically as they are visually.

Leave no trace!

What other festival in the world cleans up after itself? Where else in the world could one find thousands of intoxicated revelers and not a single empty beer bottle on the ground, or even a cigarette butt? Even if many Burners think there is "nothing there," they strive to keep it that way.

Have a great burn.

On the Playa it's more both/and than either/or. Bring it. Build it. Do it.

On the Playa

We were still setting up. A bunch of rednecks on top of a big flatbed that they thought passed as an art car were driving too fast and stirring up a bunch of dust. One of them was shouting mockingly into a bullhorn: "Hey you fuckin hippies, clean up after yourselves. Leave no trace now."

The redneck wasn't addressing anyone in particular, but Owl started waving him the bird, and then called out to him to make sure he saw it. "Hey redneck." The redneck waved it back. We were brothers after all, I guess. I'm sure he would have thrown us a beer if we'd asked.

Potlatch

> If the masses consolidate their presence on the stage of history, a new religion will emerge to take the place of the old religions administered by specialists in public consumption. It cannot be the obsolete Nature worship that conservationism is vainly trying to resuscitate. Consumption cannot not be sacrificial, and sacrifice cannot not be sacrilegious. (Brown 1991, p. 197)

To some Earth First! types, who have been visiting and camping on the Black Rock Desert for years, Burning Man is a noisy and smelly desecration of the desert. This in turn has prompted a preemptory dismissal of "Deep Ecology" by many in the younger generation of technophilic Burners. While it is true that, apart from the occasional lost invertebrate, the sink is devoid of plant and animal life forms—at least of any over one hundred micrometers—to say "but, there's nothing out there" is blasphemy to any greenish sort with even a trace of nature mysticism.

Even Larry Harvey, Burning Man's serendipitous and distinctly non-mystical founder, after stating that they moved Burning Man from Baker Beach in San Francisco to the Black Rock because it was "400 square miles of nothing," added:

> It turns out that in this vast desert space ... that there are peculiar properties, peculiar magic that takes hold. Suddenly we encountered something, it was like the ocean that had backed the Man before, this ... great sweep of nature, that's, that was always part of it. But this was an ocean you could walk on. This was a great piece of nothing in which anything that was, was more intensely so.
> (Harvey 1997)

The anti-green sentiments are not universal, by any means—in fact, the opposite is more true. Burning Man theorists almost always place themselves in the Situationist lineage. René Riesel, about as "in the Situationist lineage" as anyone could be, might just as easily be claimed by Deep Ecology:

> Radicalism means, literally, "grasping things by their roots," not rejuvenating a peremptory anticapitalism adorned with clichés from Bourdieu. What does the "left of the left"—this miscellany of citizens' groups, supporters of the Tobin tax, antiglobalists, and third-worldist holdouts, all more or less managed by former Trotskyist cadres—want? The State, more of the State. The most conscious of the young "activists" will admit that there's some theoretical work to do and that you can't make use in kit form of the old stuff available on the market, nor even hop the train of what might appear the most accomplished expression of the old critical movement at the end of the '60s: situationist theory. Grasping things by their roots means critiquing the technoscientific bases of modern society, understanding the deep ideological kinship between political or social progressivism and scientific progressivism. Since the "industrial revolution" in England, industrialization has been an absolutely fundamental rupture with the essence of the progress of humanization. (Riesel 2001)

Actually, I think that old monkey-wrencher, Hayduke, would love Burning Man.

There have even been sightings . . .

And, actually, since Riesel brought it up, the largest cadre of Trotskyists today is probably in the White House, where they are called "Neocons."

Twenty million years ago the Black Rock desert was a lake. One million years ago, after the Sierra Nevada uplift, the Black Rock desert was still a lake. Ten thousand years ago it was a lake, a great lake, two hundred miles long, fifty miles wide, and eight hundred feet deep: Lake Lahontan. You can see the beach terraces high up on the surrounding mountains. The fans at the mouths of the canyons are littered with obsidian flakes—almost anyone who hikes into the mountains can find projectile points. Some of them are quite large, and fluted—they weren't used for deer. The really old ones are basalt. One of the largest mammoth skeletons ever found was right here, above the Playa. This was "good ground." They made their boats from tule reeds.

On the Playa

Late Sunday afternoon a huge moving van and a caravan of smaller cars and trucks came rolling down 7:30 towards the Esplanade. They were blasting Cramps and psychobilly with a thousand watts. There were two naked go-go dancers on top of the van. Ubercarney had arrived from Detroit. Our neighbors.

Black Rock City was rising from the desert. Processions of cars, trucks, and vans were arriving in a steady stream. The empty blocks of Black Rock City were filling in. Radio Burning Man was up. The Man wasn't finished, but they pulled him up at night and lit him—the central beacon and orientation point. By now "Playa" referred only to the several square miles of lakebed encircled by the Esplanade—the rest was Black Rock City.

They come from Madison, Salt Lake City, Coos Bay;
Chicago, Ottawa, Seattle;
New York, Joshua Tree, Orinda;
Venice, Oakland, San Antonio;
Muscatine, Iowa, and Philadelphia, PA;
Santa Fe and Tempe;
Haleiwa, Monterey, Houston;
Washington D.C.;
Boise, Eugene, London;
Tulsa, and Lawrence.

The "Republic of China Town" came from Taipei, offering, among other things, "betelnut beauties and philanthropic gangsterism."

And the Cat Herders Union, Local 451, arrived from San Francisco.

This was gonna be a P-A-R-T-Y.

Burning Man

Burning Man evolved through the fortuitous collaboration of Larry Harvey and a loose coalition of performance artists called the Cacophony Society, first in San Francisco, and later, starting in 1990, on the alkali flats of the Black Rock Desert in Nevada. The artists might be called Dadaists, or followers of Artaud, or any number of more pejorative epithets. Certainly, they were the inheritors of the "happenings" of the Sixties, of the Living Theater of Julian Beck and Judith Malina, of artists such as Jean-Jacques Lebel in France and the Fluxus group in New York. Erik Davis, in his insightful essay "Beyond Belief: The Cults of Burning Man," astutely points out the line back to the junkyard creations of George Herms, Wallace Berman, and Simon Rodia in Los Angeles. Davis identifies five aspects of Burning Man culture, which he centers in the "Cult of Experience."

> The essential cult is the Cult of Experience, a cult to which all Burners in some sense belong. . . . [followed by] four more specific formations: the Cult of Intoxicants, the Cult of Juxtapose, the Cult of Flicker, and the Cult of Meaningless Chaos. (Davis 2005, p. 17)

Each of these aspects supports and is reflected by the others: the flicker of intoxication, the intoxication of flicker, the chaos of ironic juxtaposition, all building towards an artistic whole beyond the imagination of any of its parts.

Make it new.

One of the strongest threads in the Burning Man lineage is to Ken Kesey, the Pranksters, and the Acid Tests. (I'm not talking about whatever was or was not in Larry Harvey's mind when he burned five pounds of wood twenty years ago on Baker Beach— I'm talking Burning Man, what's happening on the Playa.)

Trippers are still the soul of the Playa.

I was going to criticize Brian Doherty, who wrote the excellent (and "officially approved") history, *This Is Burning Man,* for his mere single-paragraph acknowledgement of Burning Man's debt to the Pranksters—until I read a review of the book in the *New York Times* by Dave Itzkoff. Itzkoff accuses Doherty of "overstating [Burning Man's] philosophical connections to the counterculture movements of 1960s-era figures like Ken Kesey." The sentence in question is:

> [Stewart] Brand's Trips Festival and the Kesey movement from which it arose struck devastating blows that made chinks in consensual reality; Burning Man is now bulldozing boldly and heedlessly through those chinks and building an entire mini-civilization around some of those same impulses that inspired the Kesey scene. (Doherty 2004, p. 153)

For this sin, Itzkoff snidely wonders if "the author has left more behind than just his objectivity in the Black Rock Playa."

Huh?

The same old. The same old NY parochialism. Like he had a clue.

The connection to Kesey's group is all the more underscored by the physical presence of a number of the Pranksters on the Playa. Not to mention scores of that more obscure group, the Psychedelic Rangers. I mean, jeez, there are even several incarnations of *Further*.

OK, but ... "mini-civilization"?

On the Playa

"Where is the art?" That's what several people in our camp asked on Sunday night.

Sunday night, the first Sunday night—the sweet night, that night before the official opening of Burning Man. On Sunday night the Playa still belongs to DPW (The Dept. of Public Works, the several hundred volunteers who spend two months building, and then dismantling, the infrastructure of Black Rock City) and other Burning Man volunteers, and to those in the registered theme camps, which are supposed to be up and operating on Monday.

We were up, but as we gazed across the Playa, the question was still there: "Is there a Burning Man this year? Where is the art?"

We were showing off, showing off that we were veteran Burners who remembered this or that great year, like all veteran Burners like to do. The art was out there—sixty official pieces—we were just showing off that we knew that Michael Christian's 42-foot-high "Flock" from 2001 was *not* there, nor other installations of huge scale and tonnage. Every year is different.

The art *was* out there. Sometimes way out there, beyond the Man, beyond the Temple. And sometimes very sweet.

We stopped at a tiny white house with a white picket fence sitting all alone on the white Playa. There was a white mailbox in front. We opened the gate and went through and opened the white door and went in. The room was white. There were a few white books white-plastered on a white shelf. There was a white chair in the corner and a white bed with a white bedspread against the wall and a white nightstand beside it. I sat down on the bed and opened the drawer of the nightstand. Inside was a journal with lots of blank white pages and a pen. I hadn't written anything for a month. I picked up the pen. It came easy.

Burning Man

Burning Man is a festival and its true roots are medieval, and, further back still, archaic. The links to the Celtic "wicker man" are obvious, and it is not a great step to Maenadism. Barbara Ehrenreich, in her 1998 essay "Transcendence, Hope, & Ecstasy," notes that in sixteenth-century France, peasants spent three months of the year in carnival revelry, one day out of four, and that in seventeenth-century Spain "a total of five months of the year were devoted to saints and observed with festivals." (Ehrenreich 1998)

Historical suppression of festivals and carnival began as early as the sixteenth century, as the power elite feared that mass festivals were potential centers of insurrections—which indeed was sometimes the case. But it was the Enlightenment, the spread of Protestantism, and the rise of industrial capitalism that doomed the festivals more completely. Ehrenreich points out that neither the Bourgeois revolutions in America and France ("Reason!"), nor the Bolsheviks, were friendly to festivals. Lenin, in fact, was grateful to the capitalists for having disciplined the working class. The old marriage of radical politics and fun re-emerged in the Sixties, with the Situationists in France and the Yippies in the United States. There is, of course, nothing overtly political about Burning Man: it's a festival. Almost nobody you might question at Burning Man would be familiar, say, with Kropotkin. Which doesn't matter much. Pointedly, the journal of the French Lettrists, later taken over by the Situationists, was called "Potlatch."

On the Playa

Monday afternoon was a respite—it was the calm before the storm. I parked on a backrest in front of the Adytum, writing in my notebook and watching the parade of cyclists and pedestrians, all the crazy and colorfuls, everyone feeling good. It was not too hot, not too windy. It was just right.

> . . . a naked woman, painted silver and gold, pedaled past
> me in the desert, simultaneously balancing on a unicycle
> and playing a tuba. (Kozinets 2002, p. 30)

I thought of Venice Beach, on a Sunday, a long time ago.

Then I heard drums approaching: a slow steady beat and loud chanting. Suddenly a column of men wearing black leather g-strings marched right through our camp. The chanting sounded like all those mummy movies when someone is about to be sacrificed. In the middle of the column was a woman on a sedan chair, lifted high by the men and surrounded by nearly naked female attendants. It was Ishtar, from Pepe Ozan's opera. They were bringing their theater to the camps.

two playa beings

Potlatch

It is easy to miss how radically subversive and liberating is the simple act of excluding money.

> It is because we do not know how to consume that so much energy is spent on accumulating excrement, or money, which cannot be consumed. (Brown 1991, p. 192)

Aside from the welcome sale of ice and coffee in Center Camp, Burning Man is non-commercial. There are no vendors, and (once you are in the gate) no money changes hands. Barter is demanded only by those who "don't understand." Mostly, anything that changes hands is given—from pancakes to margaritas to bicycle parts to swag (a.k.a. "schwag," the myriad of trinkets, bracelets, decals, CDs, and glow sticks that move between the camps and the Playa). The same is true of services offered by the various camps— whether it's a ride on Ubercarney's "roller coaster," a shower, a trip to the medical tent, getting a generator fixed, getting a massage or a pubic haircut, or "blow jobs for the desperate," it's all gifted. The system depends on voluntary reciprocity—old-timers will remember the "pass it on" of the Sixties—and is a key foundation of much of the magic of Burning Man, an underlying feeling of excitement, liberation, and political hope.

> Festivals provide ritual power for inverting, temporarily overturning, and denying the currently entrenched social order of market logics, which are necessary prerequisites for consumer emancipation. (Kozinets 2002, p. 34)

Robert Kozinets published an ethnographical study of Burning Man for the *Journal of Consumer Research*, investigating Burning Man as an "anti-market event."

J F POPE

an uncentered camp

Findings reveal several communal practices that distance consumption from broader rhetorics of efficiency and rationality. (Kozinets 2002, from the abstract)

Kozinets began his research with two years of studying Burning Man literature, websites, and chat lists before he decided that he'd better do some fieldwork. Judging from some of his remarks, such as "the felt need to reciprocate," it sounds suspiciously like he "went native."

According to Kozinets, authentic participation was construed at Burning Man as not behaving like a *consumer:*

> Complaints were frequently directed at the careless, polluting, spectating nature of the people who came to the weeklong event only for the final day or two. These people were variously termed "tourists," "weekenders," "spectators," "yahoos," "lookie-loos," and "frat boys"—terms related to consumer and couch potato by their passive, visual, and socially isolated connotations. These outsiders were judged as inauthentic. (Kozinets 2002, p. 25)

Kozinets' observations do not contradict Brown: Dionysian consumption is participatory. Kozinets frequently refers to the negative effects of "the market" or, more specifically, large corporations, on community—evidently a well-known (as it certainly should be by now) and much-discussed thesis among academic consumer scientists:

> The result is a pathologizing dialectic in which an isolating consumer culture spread by exploitative large corporations sickens and undermines the norms of a caring, sharing, and civilly engaged community. (Kozinets 2002, p. 26)

Kozinets critically investigates whether the Burning Man "hyper-community" creates a viable possibility of "market emancipation."

Still, I wonder. Maybe *any* community could deal with corporate damage to their social "norms" were it not that the same corporations also engage in theft, embezzlement, bribery, ecological devastation, assassinations of political and labor leaders, wholesale massacres, and callous poisoning of wells.

Reverend Billy came with his Church of Stop Shopping. He had a full gospel choir in robes and a good fiery sermon. He even had two bodyguards, in dark suits and dark glasses and thin dark ties.

Burning Man

2004 Burning Man sold 35,000 tickets—the most ever to that time (2005 was about the same). Most Burners think that is too many. Most Burners, in fact, think that the right size is whatever size Burning Man happened to be the first year they attended. For me, that's about 8,000, but even at 20,000, I thought it was still OK. All Burners get to bitch—that's a right they earn by the days and weeks and months of unpaid preparation that they contribute to create the event.

All of the collectives have some presence: punks, grungers, the e-tribes and the tech tribes, the psychonauts, moon tribes, goddess tribes, gay tribes, meta and latex—hundreds of artistic collectives, old bohemians, the pagans and pole dancers, the sex workers, the country tribes, the mountain tribes, the urban cults and the metal cults, kick-ass groups and incense groups, ravers and savers, all outlandishly costumed, with wheeled vehicles of every conceivable construction, pedaled and motored.

Matt Wray's list:

> There are all sorts here, a living, breathing encyclopedia of subcultures: Desert survivalists, urban primitives, artists, rocketeers, hippies, Deadheads, queers, pyromaniacs, cybernauts, musicians, ranters, eco-freaks, acidheads, breeders, punks, gun lovers, dancers, S/M and bondage enthusiasts, nudists, refugees from the men's movement, anarchists, ravers, transgender types, and New Age spiritualists. (Wray 1995)

As far as I know, there are representatives of every religion of the known world (yes, there are Zoroastrians). And (it should not be surprising, given the thousands of trailers and RVs) there are Gypsies, Romani. (Black 2000) To those old enough to remember, it's a flash of hope—that again, after forty years, there could be coalition.

Fuckin hippie!

Lush Culture and Head Culture

Brian Doherty, in *This Is Burning Man*, characterizes Playa culture as a knife-edge tiptoe between "two dominant alternative outlooks in American underground culture," which he calls punk and hippie. He begins by excusing himself, saying that living at Burning Man one learns to mistrust sweeping generalizations about human types. Then he continues:

> "Punk" is the attempt to transgress perceived limits of acceptable and proper behavior and comportment through a sometimes cynically mean absurdity (redeemed by being often hilarious); "hippie" is the belief that "love is all you need" and that the proper response to American mainstream culture is a manic togetherness and all-encompassing acceptance that's all sweet and no sour—it can be inspiring but can also seem disturbingly soft and gelatinous. (Doherty 2004, p. 169)

First, in my opinion, Doherty's caricature is aimed at the teeny-boppers, not the *real* hippies.

But then, I suppose we all say that.

I guess it's just that, at the end of the day, being tough is not enough—you want some friends—that's what we learned.

But I don't agree with Doherty's dichotomy—it's not between punk and hippie—who, almost all of the time, get along just fine: giggling, laughing, sharing, getting high. The dichotomy is between lush culture and head culture. One might say that Burning Man is an experiment in mixed inebriant coexistence.

The Pharmacology of Burning Man

If the world is a drug, poetically speaking, it is not unreasonable to define a culture by its intoxicants. In the case of Burning Man, however, this is particularly difficult because of the plethora of distinctive tribal units. There are strictly beer drinkers and whiskey alcoholics, cocktail loungers, dope smokers, and huffers; pill poppers, cokeheads, and streakers; there's always the occasional junkie; there are E-heads and acid heads and the phenethylamine/tryptamine psychonauts. Who did I miss?

I gleaned the following entries from four different issues of *Piss Clear*, one of Black Rock City's "alternative" newspapers (yes, there is an "official" newspaper also):

WHAT'S OUT	WHAT'S IN
Acid	Cocaine
Beer snobs	Cold beer of any kind
GHB	Mushrooms and booze

Red Bull	Power Horse
Speed	Weed
E	2CB
E-tards	Drunkards
Beer and ludes	Acid and Viagra
Hippie crack	Crack
Cold soup out of a can	Meth diets

Now, *Piss Clear* is no more representative of the Playa than I am
. . . well . . . that may be overstating things, but still. And the
list is in fun and the inconsistencies are noted. Further, according to numerous informants, it's a little premature to say that
"hippie crack" (nitrous oxide) is "out." Still, there is nothing
on the list that is not reflected in the non-Burning Man culture
(though there is no mention of prescription painkillers, which
are probably as common at Burning Man as they are, say, in
radio broadcasting). If meth use is up, that's no different than
places like Kansas.

I should state that the Burning Man Organization does not support taking illicit drugs. They say, quite correctly, that it's crazy
enough out there.

After the first drug, the rest are mere hallucinations.

There is no typical Burner, drug-wise. The nine blind men trying to describe an elephant by the part of it they touch is nowhere
more apt. I state that as an apology and defense to the 34,999
people who will react to my micro-impressions with a "huh?"
Still, as it was one of my particular interests, a few generalizations seemed to emerge. Anyway, here is my report.

For one, teetotalers, as a group, while not absent, are underrep-
resented. There is an Anonymous Camp (for 12-Steppers) and
the CSB Camp ("clean and sober Burners"). And others, I'm
sure. But still.

The most ubiquitous drug (and the drug of choice in the two
camps named above) is, no surprise, coffee. Besides the necessary ice, it is the single item vended in Center Camp. After that,
the most widespread drug is alcohol, followed by all of those
that could loosely be called hallucinogens.

Alcohol use is probably fairly constant, but it seems to be more
dominant on Monday night and again on Saturday night, the
night of the burn. On Monday night I think that a lot of people
are still exhausted from setting up, or aren't quite set up, and
margaritas may seem more comforting than tripping. This is not
the case on Saturday, when the trippers are out in force. On Saturday night everyone is out. It may be the presence of the week-

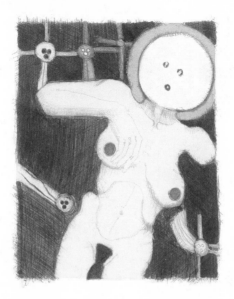

night tripping

enders (the spectators, the oglers, the frat boys, etc. etc.) that seems to give the boozers a lot of visibility.

Tuesday and Wednesday nights the "E" vibe is strong—those beautiful glow-stickers lying around the dome in little mush-piles. For those who do it, Tuesday is usually the first night of the "Psychedelic Pentathalon." For purposes of the Pentathalon, on Tuesday at least, MDMA counts as a psychedelic—even if it's not combined with something else.

J.POPE

a frat boy

By Thursday night the Playa is palpably psychedelic. Even more on Friday night, when it's an Acid Test in overdrive, multiplied a hundred-fold: massive freaking, lights and lasers, everything outlandish and over-the-top and fun and wonderful.

Sunday night nobody has come down from everything they were taking the rest of the week, and it's a mish-mash.

If there are trends, some think the boozers are increasing their numbers at a slightly higher rate than the trippers.

There is a lot of crossover, of course. Almost every tripper enjoys a swig from a flask of fine tequila, but the reverse current has never been as strong. Huge amounts of alcohol are consumed at Burning Man, given away at a hundred "lounges" and a thousand camps and on a hundred art cars. Part of the art of partying on the Playa is choosing the right art car to jump onto. If you're a tripper, you don't want to end up with a bunch of drunks.

On the Playa

On the other hand, landing on a car with a bunch of hippie-bashing *punks* is actually fun:

> *"Hey, it's some fuckin hippies."*

Owl answered them:

> *"Oh, yeah, I remember you guys. I was there. We were lined up on one side of the street to hear the Jerry Garcia Band, you punks were lined up on the other side to hear . . . the Dead Kennedys. Then one of you threw a stink bomb at us."*

Owl was stretching out into his story, using his arms and hands and pointing a finger:

> *"Now, this was new, so it took us a while to figure it all out. We'd had tear gas lobbed at us, but never a stink bomb. So we had to talk about it a lot so we could understand what was happening."*
> > *'Wow, that's a stink bomb.'*
> > *'They threw a stink bomb at us?'*
> > *'Yeah, look, it's a stink bomb.'*
> > *'Wow, they threw a stink bomb at us.'*
> > *'Yeah, wow. They threw a stink bomb at us.'*
>
> *"Everybody stared at it a bunch. One guy said:*
> > *'I'm not sure it's a stink bomb. Doesn't smell bad to me.'*

"Anyway, we talked about it a lot. Somebody asked if it we thought it was an unfriendly act."

'I mean, man, do you think that was uncool? I mean, an unfriendly act?'

'Well, I don't know if I would go THAT far, man.'

'Yeah, maybe you're right. But maybe they were trying to TELL us something.'

"So we talked about that possibility for a while. And that's why we gave you a stick of incense."

"Hey, see you in hell, hippie."

"See you in hell, punk . . . . actually, I think that bus there might be headed that way now—catch you later."

Burning Man

Burning Man must be one of the most photogenic events any-where in the world. Just the faces, bodies, and costumes could keep dozens of photographers busy for the rest of their lives, even without all the art, sets, camps, and mutant vehicles. There are a couple of excellent photographic books, one by Holly Kreuter and one published by *Hardwired* magazine, and there are scores of photographic collections on the Internet. (See "ImageGallery" at the Burning Man website, where more than six hundred photographers are listed. George Streng's portraits are particularly haunting.)

It's interesting that while good photographers have been able to catch the spirit of the day trippers, I've never seen anything that comes close to capturing what it's like on the Playa at night. At night there are the lights. And it's more about movement. And panoramic scale.

The Burning Man Organization makes no attempt to control non-commercial photography, but there are restrictions on video cameras—a permit is required. Still, some think Burning Man would be better off without *any* press coverage, that "No spectators" should mean just that. Give folks some privacy, after all.

Kind of like the Bohemian Club

On the Playa

By Wednesday morning Black Rock City has found its pace—everyone tired enough from late-night partying that people are sleeping in and the morning is quieter.

This year I was part of a camp called Delphic Delirium, organized by a couple of poets—a strikingly beautiful woman named Lolo and a grizzled half-crazed beatnik named Owl. Owl was on so many different drugs that his value as an informant was minimal—other than as being a kind of weird antenna attracting different energies in off the Playa (all welcomed by Lolo's gracious hospitality).

Their camp had constructed a thirty-foot yurt-like structure that they called "the Adytum." The huge parachute over the roof was tie-dyed, the walls were painted with petroglyphs, and the poles were glowing with a thousand feet of "cool neon" electroluminescent wire. The overall effect might be called paleo-psychedelic. They had rugs on the floor, and mattresses and pillows on the rugs. The Adytum faced due east, towards the Man, like a peyote tipi.

Some nights the musicians in the camp would have enough consciousness and will to crawl over to their amps and turn them on, to plug in their instruments, and jam. Other nights the Adytum turned into a bunch of mini mushpiles.

Delphic Delirium has an open mic—both the conversations and the music are meant to be interactive and amped back to the Playa—the idea being that the true Oracle is the crazy stuff that stumbles in through the door. Sometimes this worked great and small miracles were not uncommon; other times it could get weird.

Wednesday night turned into a conversation night. Friends of Owl's and Lolo's kept dropping by and subjects varied widely from science to philosophy to the nature of Burning Man to the nature of inspiration to the nature of nature. That kind of night. A lot of time seemed to be spent rolling around laughing.

A guy walked in—an easy-going affable Burner type—and joined our circle. The conversation hadn't seemed particularly weird to me, but all of a sudden the guy I was talking to, this nice-seeming guy that had just walked in, the way we liked people to do, began to get panicky. I could see that his brain was beginning to short-circuit, and suddenly a horrifying idea flashed through what was left of his brain and he jumped up.

"Is everyone here on acid?"

On reflection, it wasn't an unreasonable question—just one that came from so far out of the past that it took a few moments for everyone to recover and consider. Everyone looked everyone else over very carefully. Finally someone was able to answer with a definitive "no." Maybe the guy had been smoking pot. I *did* remind him that he was in Delphic Delirium. That didn't comfort him any. He'd just walked in and talked and listened and now he was insane. How had we dosed him? He looked suspiciously at a water bottle and ran away.

Sometimes it was like that. Just a bunch of people sitting around laughing and talking.

Merry was telling Playa stories, about Space Lounge, and Flight to Mars, and other places he'd been. Then he said, "You've probably heard the rumor of the woman with the pierced clitoris who ripped out her ring when she accidentally caught it on something— twice, actually—well, here's the true story." And he told it, and how, after all of it, he had reinserted the ring. He told Sandra to show it to us, and Sandra dutifully pulled up her skirt, opened her legs and spread her labia and we all looked. And sure enough, there it was. At least I think that was what I was looking at.

One night about an hour before dawn a tall guy with a bit of a chip on his shoulder looked in the entrance and asked, "So where's the delirium?" Lolo giggled and told him to come in. He started to, then froze, perhaps sensing among the fifteen innocent-looking Burners an undercurrent of danger. His caution got the better of him and he turned around and left.

We should post a sign: "Minds messed with here."

People with attitude, we liked to mess with them, particularly.

We seemed to attract more than our share of newbies—we got the sweet ones—the kid who saved and borrowed, whose friends covered for him while he was gone, just so he could, for the first time in his life, do something for himself and by himself—something that might help him find a new life (his friends "covering

an innocent man

for him" included moving his things out of one apartment and into another while he was here at Burning Man!).

Every night had its own particular character—on music nights a jazz musician might drop in and turn everything in a new direction, or someone trying to find their voice might get so completely lost at the microphone that they required extreme acoustic wakeup.

Lolo graciously welcoming a visitor

The camp people were a pretty strange group, but it was a perfect place for my research and I am grateful to Lolo and Owl for letting me be part of their camp.

Burning Man

Almost the first thing I ever saw at Burning Man was a large banner saying "No Spectators." In spite of the fact that, in the best Burning Man spirit, a group founded "Spectator Camp," erecting a grandstand on the Esplanade, this rule has wide support, as does "No Vending" and "Leave No Trace." The "No Vending" rule now extends to a general anti-market ethos— participants are encouraged to mask the large corporate logos on rented trucks and vans.

There are a few other rules too, such as "No Guns" and "No Explosives." The "No Guns" rule wasn't added until 1997 (at some of the older burns there was actually a "drive-by shooting range"). Of course there is a hard-core cadre that believe that all of Burning Man's current problems, such as police walking unannounced into people's camps, would be solved if the rule were rescinded.

And all other rules, for that matter. Goddammit.

(And for some reason, at the end of such a rant, someone will blame the "fuckin hippies").

There are other rules that go along with the mottos of "Radical Self-Expression" and "Radical Self-Reliance," and occasional conflicts are inevitable. In 1999, due to continuing complaints from their neighbors and an uncompromising attitude, the Capitalist Pigs Camp was actually ejected from the Playa. (As a last spiteful gesture, in a sort of "scorched earth" policy, the "Pigs" set fire to a huge pile of their chairs, couches, mattresses, and plastic tarps, smothering several blocks of the City with toxic smoke.)

Anarchism does not mean (and has never meant) that there are no rules. "No ruler" is closer. Anarchism means that the basis of the society is cooperation rather than coercion. You have to get along with your neighbors. If you are too loud and you tell your neighbors to fuck off, DPW will arrive with their one thousand watts of snarling attack dogs blaring. If your neighbors think that your art is too damn offensive, it is—move it somewhere else. That's anarchism in action. (That is *not* the same thing as the Sheriff ordering a sign removed because *he* thinks it is offensive. Why is this so hard to understand?)

Three guys, dressed in clean and pressed business suits, carrying briefcases and each talking into a cell phone, walked briskly past us down the Esplanade.

"Curiouser and curiouser," mumbled Alice.

The Better Humour Ice Cream Truck. The Mud Bath Hole. The Maze. The BookMobile.

On the Playa

A guy in a postal uniform came in. He was from the Black Rock Post Office. He was holding a post card. "Is there an 'Owl' here?"

Owl stood up. He was wearing a penis gourd and moccasins.

The guy looked at him.

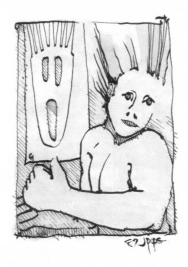

Black Rock City postman

"I need three pieces of ID."

It took half an hour of discussion on the meaning of "identity" and the socially constructed nature of "proof," along with bribes of cheese, apple, and soda, to get the card. It was from another member of the camp: "Having wonderful time. Wish you were here."

Starlight's Casbah

Starlight had a large tent. On the outside she had painted all manner of slithering and reptilian creatures, dream animals— some of them had legs and extra eyes and spots and all of them seemed to be glowing from the glitter she had mixed with her paints. Tension ropes crossed the long sides to stabilize it and hold it down in the wind.

Inside it was like a Turkish palace. Beautiful fabrics hung from the roof of the tent and draped the sides. The floor was covered with pads and cushions. Glowing cool neon electroluminescent wire outlined the windows and corners and gave the whole room a soft light. There was an antique hookah in one corner and multiple feeds from a blue nitrous tank were placed around the cushions. Starlight was draped with a sparkling see-through fabric. I had found the garden of earthly delights.

Owl was lying on his back in a corner, talking about Kant to nobody in particular.

Potlatch

> The human tendency that Bataille sees at work in the potlatch is not aggression but death: the need to lose, the need to spend, to give away, to surrender; the need to sacrifice. (Brown 1991, p. 187)

Brown points out that, with the death of God, "the scholar of one candle feels afraid." That Protestantism-capitalism has carried the masochistic logic to new levels, "piercing the soul far more deeply than any Roman Catholic penitential exercises."

And since Luther and Calvin desacralized human life, conspicuous consumption could no longer be for the glory of God. Simultaneously, there was an elevation of asceticism—God to be worshipped through the denial of simple human pleasures.

> The glorification of God by the nullification of man carries the masochistic potential of religion to a new level: our nullification, our humiliation as worthless creatures in the sight of God, is our sanctification. After the death of God the theology of human nullity becomes the pathology of nihilism. (Brown 1991, p. 189)

If you (sadistically) scratch it, masochism is never far beneath the surface of the Dionysian potlatch (or, for that matter, its contrary twin, Christianity).

Spanking Camp
Princess Reform School
Advanced Rope Bondage
7 Sins Spanking Wheel
Playfully Yours
The Sensual Side of Dungeon Play
Slave Sale for Homos
Temple of Atonement
Blood Fetishes

And it seems quite natural that the more extreme forms of rave dancing—those Kali-worshipping Goa trancers—have made the Playa a second home.

The stretch to death may seem like a long one (for Brown, it's through Freud), but we can get some help from Barbara Ehrenreich. In her book *Blood Rites: Origins and History of the Passions of War,* Ehrenreich is looking at the history, and pre-history, of war and our feelings about it, and she begins with blood sacrifice. Ehrenreich is not a Freudian, as Brown is; thus it is all the more interesting that they arrive at such similar positions:

> Capitalism has proven itself more dynamic—i.e., Dionysian—than socialism. (Brown 1991, p. 189)

> Ultimately, twentieth-century socialism lost out to nationalism for the same reason the universalistic, post-axial religions did: It has no blood rite at its core, no thrilling spectacle of human sacrifice. (Ehrenreich 1997, p. 224)

Sacrifice has a double face: *sacer* (sacred) and accursed.

> The human sacrifices of Aztecs, Islamic jihad, Tibetan monasteries of Buddhist contemplation, as well as potlatch, are all seen as alternative ways of obeying the imperative social need to squander wealth. . . . as if the proper thing to do with the economic surplus (painfully accu-

> mulated by economic sacrifices) is to give it away; and
> as if gods exist to receive it—i.e., that religion is essen-
> tially the theater of masochism. (Brown 1991, p. 188)

It should not be surprising that out of the thousands and tens of thousands of revelers, one or two have mistaken themselves for the god and walked naked into the fire. It actually stamps the ceremony as genuine. (Human sacrifice was not unknown at the old potlatches either. Nor at the Celtic wicker man. Euripides would have left it in.)

This world was, is, and always will be, everliving fire.

Dionysus, the god of madness, is also death.
—Heraclitus

A man who knew something about fire.

On the Playa

Wednesday there was a white-out dust storm, where visibility is reduced to three or four feet. Everything tends to freeze in place: the art cars have to stop and park, bicycles have to be

Jah and Snooker

walked, and walking involves leaning. Two Bedouin-looking figures, scarves wrapped around their heads and faces, white from head to toe, emerged from the dust. It was Jah and Snooker.

Jah and Snooker had ridden out to the extreme edge of the Burning Man encirclement—past the Man, past the Temple of Stars, and beyond that all the way to the orange trash fence. Just to go there and to be on the edge of the world. Then a bus had driven by—a very cool-looking bus. So they parked their bikes and climbed on board.

It was a cool bus, but it was headed back to Center Camp, and about the time they got there, a dust storm set in and the bus parked. They had to walk the several miles back out to where they had left their bikes, and then walk them back. All in the fury of the dust storm.

Snooker's face looked like a Butoh dancer, completely white from a thick layer of dust. He was laughing. He'd just been on the greatest walk of his life.

Near dusk, the wind died down.

Getting Laid

My girlfriend came back to the tent. She'd been out watching men stroke other men's penises. "They were so . . . gentle." Her eyes had a dreamy, faraway look. Home-fucking is not always the same thing as getting laid. At Burning Man it's kind of a collateral plus.

"Especially for those over fifty," she added, demurely.

On the Playa

There is an underlying erotic energy that pulses across the Playa—it's not everywhere and it's not all the time, but it's always close by, submerging and re-emerging, there, here, never far away. Sometimes it is explicit, as with the pole dancers and the go-go dancers in their cages—sometimes it's an understory, as with the see-through blouses, the painted body parts, the nudity.

One year we were camped next to the spanking camp and the barker was driving us crazy with his nasty insinuating voice. We didn't really want to go out—it was cuddle time for us—but out we had to go. No place we passed looked inviting—it was all looking like Coney Island or the Las Vegas strip—we were trapped in nightmare Babylon. Didn't anyone else on the Playa take *good drugs*?

And there, back a short distance off the Esplanade, a naked man and a naked woman were dancing. A woman was singing and a man was playing digeridoo. It was the most erotic dance I had ever seen. They were dancing Desire. They were dancing Wanting. It was what all the sham dancing at sex clubs pretended to. It was real, it was private, it was personal, and they were gifting us.

Potlatch

> A sacred act must involve violence and rupture, breaking the boundary. (Brown 1991, p. 197)

For all of its artistic and cognitive violence, physical violence is most remarkable for its absence—a contradiction that would not have surprised Blake at all. For all of the nudity, exhibitionism, prurience, and intoxication, it is the rarity of rape, assault, or even fisticuffs that stands out. (The Sixties were *not* like this.)

The violence of Burning Man is transgressive, iconoclastic. For a collection of 30,000 revelers, many of them intoxicated, partying, celebrating anarchy and freedom, this lack of physical mayhem should make anyone wonder "what is going on?"

Officially, there has never been a rape at Burning Man. Several threads on eplaya.com, a discussion site for Burners, report that rapes have indeed occurred—mostly with Rophynol. The women chose not to report them. In one case a couple spent months tracking down the perpetrator and had him arrested. Much of the discussion revolved around how to handle the problem within the community.

The rites of Dionysus, where joy, abandon, licentiousness, and freedom mix with risk, danger, blasphemy, and excess, are best seen as prophylaxis. The Greeks certainly understood them thus. That, in the present century, these rites find themselves coupled to a celebration of fire should not be surprising.

On the Playa

A very sweet-looking young woman, twenty-something, asked the way to Asylum.

"They're having a muff-diving demonstration."

There was a pause.

"Do you know what that is?"

There was no irony in her voice. She was really asking. The gray hairs in my beard couldn't have been showing through the alkali dust that coated them . . . what was it?

She was wearing a demure white blouse and some kind of rabbit skin-looking things wrapped around her thighs. She'd left her cute blond snatch just enough room to peek out at the wind. I stared at it.

"No," I said, "what's muff-diving?" Just in case she didn't get the message I added, "Looks pretty nice down there."

The dear thing smiled. Beamed, really. It was like she'd just gotten a compliment from Daddy, I guess. My girlfriend wandered over. I put my arm around her and slipped it down into her pants to feel her butt.

"Hey, ever heard of 'muff-diving'?"

Burning Man

Owl walked in from the Esplanade, where he'd been talking to two guys in duck suits. He shook his head. "They're not anarchists," he said, "they're Libertarians!"

"Bigot," I said.

The "A" word comes up frequently in discussions of Burning Man theorists. For many Burners, anarchism is equated with license—"hey, there are no rules here, I can say 'fuck,' I can *write* FUCK on a big sign." And they do. They complain that people saying "down in front" at the Opera or at the Burn are "Playa Fascists" who are ruining their burn. Still, almost everyone "gets it." That the heart of Burning Man is community.

Sign taped to one porta-potty:

> *I don't care how stoned you are or bombed, or wasted, Keep the potty clean. —Steve the Camp Fascist*

After stepping into one of the porta-potties and, for the fifth time in a row, finding the seat covered with pee, I called to the guy who had just left. "Hey, did you just *use* this?" He looked back, surprised. "Oh, sorry man," and cleaned off the seat.

> *Sad, a generation that's never been in prison, or even the army— they think it has to do with Mom.*

Hugh D'Andrade, in the *Burning Man Journal* ("All the news that's fit to burn"), writes:

> In the absence of the civilizing influence of community, a vision of social life emerges in which individuals compete mercilessly against each other; cooperation and

> openness are seen as signs of weakness, and the pursuit
> of power, wealth and status appears to be the only goal of
> life. (D'Andrade 2004)

D'Andrade, mistakenly, in my opinion, states that to call this
tendency "conservative" is a misnomer.

> Nothing truly democratic is conserved by policies that
> plunder the environment, diminish public services, limit
> civil liberties, and burden future generations with the
> weight of debt. (D'Andrade 2004)

Curtailing the "excesses of democracy" has been a central part
of the conservative agenda at least since the time of Hamilton.

D'Andrade ends his article with the graffito from Paris, 1968:

> *Be realistic—Demand the impossible.*

On the Playa

The Feely Box is built a little larger than a phone booth with
kind of a steeple on top—which gives it more the appearance of
a miniature chapel than an outhouse. There are three arm holes
cut into each side at various heights, so that one can put an arm
in through the red velvet sleeve and touch whoever is inside
without being able to see them.

a puja goddess

LuckyCharms said that when he reached in he touched a guy's back. Then he reached in his other arm and it was another naked back but not a guy. They had their arms around each other and there were really sweet moaning sounds and then the whole box was humping and rocking.

"When we first decided to do this for our project this year none of us imagined that we would actually get volunteers to be inside the box . . . . Imagine our surprise when we would actually have a line of people waiting to get their turn inside."
—Mistress of Mirth

Katrina said that what she touched inside was a very "manly" man. She said she had such a good time she went back and did it again. Friendly Jen did it twice, also.

Julie C said that she had just come from Extreme Elvis, and that after his "dinky Dinky," what she felt up in the booth was "most welcome, and restored my faith in humanity."

After Lothar felt up a giggling woman inside, he "had a smile on his face for the next hour."

> "What should we do?"
> "I dunno, we could go to the Feely Box."

Or we could go see what's happening at Lumerian Dolphin Tribe, the erotic goddess specialists.

There was a tantric sex camp that had a huge pair of red lips as the entrance to their tent, vertical, like in the poem by Ana Rosetti. They accepted both couples and singles for their training, but only a very few at a time. The training was "hands on," or whatever phrase one might come up with. A few people were sitting out in front waiting their turn. They only operated for a few hours each day and night, and by mid-week the reservation list was completely full.

Burning Man

The key to Burning Man is participation. This year, a carpenter friend who had cruised Burning Man for a few years as an unabashed spectator made himself a "spirit stick"—a stout staff adorned with feathers and animal skulls.

It was the first time that I'd gone out and walked around. Another guy with a spirit stick saw me and raised his up in the air and waved. People were giving me stuff and talking to me.

It doesn't take a lot to join in. I've seen lots of middle-aged folks who have parked a small trailer somewhere in the outer circles. They always do something: even if it's just laying down Astroturf and putting up a little picket fence and some of those silly wooden pinwheel flowers and a few lawn chairs.

The wife and I wouldn't spend our vacation any other way.

A seventy-three-year-old woman who attended Burning Man for the first time reported that she "had a blast."

According to the "Black Rock Bureau of Statistics," slightly over a third of the participants are between the ages of thirty and forty. The other two-thirds are evenly divided above and below.

Zazen on the Playa

At six o'clock most of us would bicycle out to the Black Rock Playa Zendo, out near the Man, for zazen. The head monk, a wild-looking saddhu, had made a large yin-yang circle that we sat around, with a Sort-Of-Buddhist altar in the center. Just outside the circle a naked woman was doing slow tai chi. Even out there it wasn't quiet and the zazen was challenging. Hundreds of bodhisattvas, some whistling, some shouting, some exploding, did their best to awaken us to true nature.

Once, on the way back to camp I stopped to have tea ceremony with the Red Monk. I think my face was already painted and glittered. He laid down cloths, offered a candy, and whisked up the tea. I drank it all in one slow draught. It was strong. He'd made it with vodka.

Do Whatever It Is You Do

At Alien Sex Camp they said they'd give me a free drink, but that first I had to dance, or tell a story, or juggle, or *"Do whatever it is you do."*

OK guys, look, I've never told anybody this before, but the truth is, the frightening truth, is that I don't really do anything. All my life I have been surrounded by artists, actors, poets, jugglers, dancers—everybody WAS somebody—everybody seemed to KNOW. And I'd just sit there, and I'd be wondering, "What is it I do, what is my 'thing'?"

(Somebody tried to interrupt me, but I've learned a *few* things in all these years. . . .)

So one day it occurred to me that being someone who didn't really "do" anything wasn't all bad. I mean, nothing is where every-

thing comes from, if you think about it. And if nothing is where everything comes from, and I'm doing nothing, then I'm doing something. Jacob Boehme thought so. Now, let me tell you about Jacob Boehme. . . .

They gave me a drink. I *think* it was Alien Sex Camp . . . Or maybe it was Space Lounge . . . Or maybe. . . .

On the Playa

A poor excuse for an art car with some kind of platform on it went by.

punk, with familiar

Hey, fuckin hippies
(Yuk, yuk, yuk)
Take a bath.
(Yuk, yuk, yuk)
Too bad you're so hard to light.
(Yuk, yuk, yuk.)

Even Jah, too young to have even been a teeny-bopper, was mystified:

"What is that about? Are we like the elders or something—like parents or something that they have to rebel against?"

owl

The car had a sign on it: "I came here to drink beer and kick ass, and I'm almost out of beer."

"Probably alky and meth," Owl said, "another Hell's Angel Wannabe."

Then he shouted out after them:

> *"Hey, you wanna be tough? Go read about JOE HILL, there was a tough guy. That is, if you CAN read."*

They were gone but Owl was just getting warmed up.

> *"You're a bigot and bigots can't make good art. Never have, never will. Go on, prove me wrong. Else curl up with your beers and*

those wimpy pills you call 'drugs' and flame your little ass-farts to the sky."

They were really gone, so Owl just said the rest of it to us: "I mean, hey, Charlie Manson was one of 'ours,' and it's nothing to be proud of."

The rednecky camps never tire of reminding people that Burning Man is *not* a Rainbow Gathering. Actually, there are always a lot of Rainbow Tribers present, lots of them around the Oregon Country Fair camp and the Green Tortoise Camp.

FUZZ—The Law

Maybe I just don't remember, but it seems like the police used to try to keep a low profile at Burning Man—to bust flagrant violations of the law but, otherwise, to try to blend in with the spirit of the event and to let the Black Rock Rangers, Burning Man's own volunteer constables, handle as much as they could. Which, generally, wasn't that much.

Police presence increased dramatically in 2000—and that was the first year that I saw "stings," plainsclothes officers who would ask some kid with a backpack if he had any weed, and then, if he said "sure," bust him.

There was that cop in his car watching the massage tables at Camp Sunscreen through his binoculars.

Still, that year the police were mostly local—deputies of the Pershing County sheriff. And, again, as I remember it, they mellowed out as the week went on and they understood that this was not like the County Fair where there would be fights and a lot of mayhem.

In 2004 there were more cops than ever—especially Feds—a trend that continued in 2005. The BLM must have scoured the cities or borrowed from the DEA because there was a host of undercover agents and some of them had that physical attitude that one expects in the inner city or in the parking lot at a Dead show, but not out on public land. This was the first year that I heard stories of police violence.

The guy was really enjoying himself.

There were undercover Feds in costumes, one with a clown face, going around trying to trade acid for some mushrooms, then busting anyone who he could get to agree. There were even Feds on art cars, asking anyone who jumped on if they had any dope to smoke. There were police using night goggles to spy on people on the Playa who were lighting pipes. Despite Burning Man's "No Dogs" rule there was a K-9 unit to sniff out marijuana. Accounts on eplaya told of police entering private camps to order "offensive" art to be removed. Peeing on the Playa was enough of an offense to warrant a search. A gay couple who had oral sex

fuzz art car (do not offer drugs)

inside one of the lounges were handcuffed and arrested and taken to jail when they stepped outside. Several people on eplaya reported police hassling foreign nationals in their camps.

Most of the drug offenders are given citations, usually a $250 fine, and the police let you know that they are doing you a favor—that if you make any trouble they'll just arrest you instead.

The Burning Man Organization, usually having to fight for their own continued existence, has been unable to raise much of a protest over the arrests. On the contrary, perhaps hoping that things won't get worse, they claim to have an "excellent" relationship with law enforcement.

In 2001, the Pershing County sheriff ordered that a painting of two men engaged in sodomy be removed from Center Camp. The owners of the painting, Camp Jiffy Lube, complied, but there was a large protest of Black Rock citizens the next day. Larry Harvey, trying both to appease the protesters and not criticize the police said, "The last thing the police want to do is to make decisions of artistic judgment." This is shockingly naïve. Of course the police want that power—it is in the nature of power to want that power—*even if most of the individual officers of that power could care less.*

Personally, I don't think that civil liberties have ever been maintained by "cooperating" with those who abrogate them. In the long run (or even in the short run), appeasement won't work. Coercive forces must be resisted—either actively or passively.

Of course, it's easy for me to say that "radical self-expression" includes blasphemy and the worship of Dionysus—I'm just a writer—I don't have to negotiate with three levels of government officials to get a permit. And the Constitutional right to free speech in print is far less eroded than is the right of peaceable assembly.

"Meanin' no disrespect, Gen'l, Suh, but don't you think . . ."

In 2006 the Burning Man Organization asked Burners to write letters to the BLM to protest yet further fee increases for expanded law enforcement. They note that between 1998 and 2004 the cost of law enforcement, which must be paid by Burning Man, rose 616 percent, while the increase in the Black Rock City population was only modest and the number of crimes in some years actually decreased.

> We should not conclude from this that Burning Man has at all lost its sacred spark. As the vampiric tendrils of consumer media and the surveillance society wrap themselves ever more tightly around the heart of human experience, the festival continues to successfully ride the paradox of regulating a temporary autonomous zone. (Davis 2003, p. 38)

On the Playa

It was Wednesday night, very late. Owl was improvising a long riff about nitrous oxide—he was mic'd so it was going out over the Playa—and a guy in a police costume stepped in. I mean, he had a vest on that said "POLICE" and he had the walkie-talkie and the Batman utility belt that they always wear. I was wondering why anyone would dress up like that—it looked too much like a real cop. Owl kept talking.

"Hello Officer, this is a drug information resource center. Out of compassion for my fellow citizens I've personally tried them all. You may ask me any question you'd like."

Owl must have been coming down. Whatever he had taken must have been shorter-acting than what I was on. Either that or he was still tripping so heavily that the presence of a cop was just one more perfect element in the whole zany tapestry. The cop, evidently, didn't see anything he could bust—perhaps he had heard of the First Amendment—and disappeared back out onto the Playa, where the sky was just beginning to lighten in the east.

Braveheart picked up a djembe, and Owl started a new song:

I just LOVE being high,
That's what the moon says.
That's what the moon says.

Lolo started singing her ethereal chorus and Jah came in with the jews harp, his intricate combinations of oscillators and feedback and electronic effects soon creating a swirl of sound whose origin quite palpably moved around over our heads.

That's what the moon says.

Nostalgia

All Burners lament the passing of when things were "really free" at Burning Man. It just seems to be part of being a Burner. I won't try to be different. My own unscientific poll, with a small "n," found a unanimous perception that at Burning Man 2004

a question of taste

there was less nudity, a lot less public sex, less blasphemy, and more highly offensive police intrusion.

And I miss the massive statements of *truly* bad taste—the pornographic and the heretical.

Like that big billboard of Jesus butt-fucking an altar boy.

There *should* be extremes that are in bad taste. Extremes by definition are in bad taste. You have to allow that. That's what tolerance is. And tolerance is the basis of any kind of free society. And the only hope for people who want to live without Big Brother.

In response to the police crackdown on public sex, Harvey, in a weak moment we hope, called public sex "inherently uncivil . . .

in the worst possible taste" and says it would be fine with him to ban it officially. (Doherty 2004, p. 230)

Where was the Blue Light District? Where was the Mustang Stud Farm?

I kind of like occasional acts of public lewdness. A little bit of real obscenity and indecency actually makes me feel more secure. I get nervous always being on the extreme by myself. Public acts of sex or penis fondling all add to the "wow, I'm not in Kansas anymore" feeling.

We'd been out bicycling with Mona. When we passed the Stud Farm there was a guy lounging on the porch. He was wearing a cowboy hat and was at attention. Mona stuck her tongue out of the side of her mouth, made a big circle, and waved us goodbye.

Truly poor taste—most of commercial America is in truly poor taste. A big house built on the very top of a hill—that's poor taste. Glen Canyon Dam, that's pretty poor taste. Suburban sprawl covering some of the best farmland in the world—that's poor taste. Huge prisons with barbed wire and guard towers—that's poor taste. Most of television—that's pretty poor taste. But a little public lewdness? Give me a break! WHO REALLY CARES?

Well, actually, a whole lot of people do. Quite viscerally, too. And with lots of self-righteousness and sincerity.

Let's just say that acts of undercover entrapment are "inherently uncivil and in the worst possible taste." And that snooping is downright unneighborly.

Sigh. In the old days, the Cops Camp served coffee and donuts. ...

Now folks are saying there should be a *Cop Watch Camp*.

"Radical self-expression" has to include some bad taste. A Festival of Fools, by ancient tradition, is where that which is not permitted is performed, where that which cannot be spoken is shouted, and where every sort of offensive sentiment, including blasphemy, is expressed. That is what makes it pleasing to the god and a protection of the people against disasters.

In ancient times, when people understood these things better, Burning Man would have been given a grant, from the Defense Department. In gold.

Dream on.

On the Playa

Treak and Mona had arrived on Thursday afternoon. I was helping them set up their tent and shade. I think they were fighting.

Mona acted quickly to set camp rules: "So if either of us is going to have sex with somebody else, you don't do it here in our tent, OK, shall we make that our rule?"

Mona

Treak muttered something that I didn't hear, and Mona responded.

"When I do it, I do it for charity. All for charity."

Mona was her Playa name. "Hi, I'm Mona Lisa." Then she'd smile.

Dream on. Dream on.

Burning Man

Nah, don't come to Burning Man. You probably won't like it. It's too dusty. It's too hot. It's too loud. The weather can be inclement. A white-out dust storm can last all day. There's a lot of jerks out there. The simplest things get harder and harder to do. If you set anything down you can never find it again. Your whole world could depend on being able to locate a spoon. There's not a single item that's not covered with white dust. By the end you'll have no brains left. You'll end up looking like one of those anti-drug ads. And I don't want to be responsible for you—I'm having trouble figuring out what I did with my water bottle.

On the Playa

Thursday night we were all out. Jah and Snooker and Scarlett. Treak and Mona were out somewhere. The Bees had all left together and were out, buzzing. Rob and Imogene were out with the Bees. Demeter was out. Pigtails was out. I cruised back around midnight but the Adytum was quiet. It was lit but the instruments were all covered. There were couples and small groups on the mattresses with the blankets pulled over them.

I asked Owl in the morning where he'd been.

"Mom and Dad decided to take the night off," he said. "We needed some time in our tent."

Baby, I want to cuddle, so bad.
Baby, I want to cuddle, so bad.

Don't want to go anywhere,
Don't want to see anything,
Just want to lie right here
And drift with our scene.

Potlatch

> It may well be that human beings can tolerate the
> Dionysian truth only if it is held at a distance, projected
> onto human or divine scapegoats, admitted under the
> sign of negation. (Brown 1991, p. 198)

Chögyam Trungpa once mused that the Yippie escapades at
Chicago were why we got Richard Nixon. Richard J. Evans, in
The Coming of the Third Reich, notes that Hitler and the National
Socialists got significant support from middle-class women, a
backlash vote against the loose sexual morals of the Weimar
Republic's artistic avant-garde—Brecht and the whole cabaret
"scene." They didn't like the movies of the new cinema (they
couldn't understand them) and they didn't like the music (jazz
played by Negroes). Hitler promised to put an end to such
shenanigans, and middle-class women voted for him in droves—
"to save their daughters."

We are *still* suffering under the backlash from the Sixties (which,
entering the mainstream, were called the Seventies). In the mid-

Seventies, if you remember, the President of the United States was calling for the decriminalization of marijuana. The frat boys haven't forgotten or forgiven the (temporary) toppling of their prestige. Dick Cheney was studying voting patterns for the Republicans while his classmates at Madison were outside being tear-gassed, protesting the war. Paul Wolfowitz, rejected by the New Left because of his Trotskyite obsession with violence, now gets to smirk. The whole ironic story is acutely chronicled by Thomas Frank in *What's the Matter with Kansas?*

But consider the fact that even civil disobedience, which is certainly "in your face," is somehow not *morally* reprehensible, even to the person who orders the protesters to be executed—it's a political matter. Defending a Dionysian orgy is trickier—a Dionysian orgy is immoral almost by definition. All of our (Apollonian) training rises up in offense.

Does that mean that Brecht and the cabaret crowd should have censored themselves, should have been less provocative? It might . . . that possibility *must* be considered. But what else can Burning Man do, and still be Burning Man? The event is *not* televised. The event takes place once a year in the middle of the most "god-forsaken" and inhospitable location in the United States. The rest of the year we're citizens. It's *Carnival*, man.

The Invasion

Somehow all of the musicians had wandered in. It was around midnight. The djembes were whaling away and Owl had started a song:

> *If you want it you can have it*
> *If you want it you can have it*

A young woman started dancing and several others joined her.

> *If you want it you can have it*
> *'Cause baby, tonight it's free*

Suddenly a drum band with horns, xylophone, and uniforms came marching down the Esplanade and right into the Adytum and filled every inch of space. Jah turned up the volume on the amps but it was no use, we were upstaged. Owl was rolling around on the ground laughing hysterically. When the band finally left and we were just starting to play again a pirate ship, streaming Jolly Rogers and aglow with lights and flashers, stopped out on the Playa. Pirates with painted faces and cutlasses leapt over the sides and ran howling towards us. No one was injured.

On the Playa

The next day was a scorcher. We stopped at the Nose to get misted and fanned, then we went back out, biking along the

Esplanade. We were just wandering, *dérive.* Then we saw it—a giant refrigerator truck, the big kind.

There was almost no line. It was dark inside but our eyes gradually opened. A DJ was spinning, but not loud. A hostess showed us to two empty folding chairs, and a waitress brought us two pink daiquiris.

Later that afternoon was the Critical Tits Ride: 6,001 naked and painted breasts biking around Burning Man in a parade that takes forty-five minutes to pass.

The party after the ride is pretty famous. Sugar Pine was supposed to stop by Delphic Delirium to sit in on a couple of sets that night, but he never made it. He had one of the coveted male invitations. "We all had to be dressed like servants. Man, do I know what it's like to be groped."

Dream on. Dream on.

Jake stopped by. He was also camping at Critical Tits. "I spent the whole day painting breasts." From our camp only Lolo joined the ride. Owl painted her.

Juumie took ecstasy for her first time—she'd never been high on *anything*—and was wholly converted:

"I've never felt so much love in my whole life."

Potlatch

> Let me unshackle the leash that keeps me safe. That protects me from myself, that makes youth long for war.
> (John Kelly, in Kreuter 2002, p. 51)

Living with some risk makes me feel more alive. I'm not saying that I'm against safety, or even security, or that I want *more* risk. There is already plenty of risk. But the attempt to eliminate *all* risk usually destroys what it was you were trying to protect in the first place. The Burning Man Organization takes all basic measures for safety, but there is a lot of dangerous stuff going on. It's a true wonder that there are so few injuries—none in 2004.

When Jean-Jacques Lebel, who was putting on "happenings" in France, was asked in 1966 if he was worried that they could result in trouble and in people getting hurt, he answered:

> No, because you have to risk something and you have to believe in a certain type of magic. You have to have faith. If you have faith in what's going to happen, you have to risk. If you're not going to go into that zone where you don't know what's going to happen, nothing's going to happen—the usual shit is going to happen. You have to let the elements go, the elements being the people with emotions and things to say, and let them express themselves. I think that's what unintentionality is—Cage's idea of indeterminacy. (Jean-Jacques Lebel 1967)

In Brown's system, risk is Dionysus. Dionysian energy has its own violence—it's transgressive by nature—and Brown was against the attempts of many to sanitize Dionysian energy. But he was steadfast that the suppression of the Dionysian influence is far more damaging and far more tragic than the wreckage characteristic of the passage of the young god himself.

For the rites of Dionysus, waste, fire, licentiousness, risk, and drug-induced madness, are seemly. Burning Man is an experiment in healing, and it should be considered one of our current National Treasures.

Have a good burn.

On the Playa

For "true" Burners (if there is such a thing) Friday night is party night. I mean, every night is party night but every night the energy keeps building. And Saturday night is the *burn* and so that's different and that leaves Friday—when everything that is ever going to be up and flashing is up and flashing. The giant lasers are on, filling the sky with criss-crossing patterns. Everyone is out—all 35,000 of them. Hundreds of weird floats and vehicles and giant tricycles are moving around on the Playa. Everything and everyone is lit and moving: light bulbs of all sorts and colors, glow sticks, glow rope, and electroluminescent wire with sequencers and controllers making fish, butterflies, a galloping puma, a jumping kangaroo—with greens and violets and yellows that make it like walking through an ayahuasca vision.

Fireworks and rockets shoot up from a dozen locations, and you can hear the deep booming from the raves at the big sound camps a mile away. Black Rock City is alive. The Man's in the center, and the City stretches in a three-mile arc of light and sound around it.

I saw the Scarlet Woman walking
Towards me from a cloud of dust.

It is Babylon the Great, reborn, arisen from the dust.

Hallucinating on the Playa

I was out with Lolo and Owl. We were trying to find Jupiter. We'd found the installations that represented all the inner planets; and then, with some difficulty, we'd found Mars, and now we were trying to find Jupiter. I was thinking that the artist had probably tried to maintain the correct relative distances, so I was looking for 5 AU, and I thought we were about there.

We were standing around a large steel sculpture—off around 4:30 but still deep in the Playa—maybe halfway between the

Esplanade and the Man. The sculpture was completely different in style from the other pieces but there was certainly something Jovian about it. Then I saw a Waorani warrior standing
out in the darkness. He had the big feathered headdress and
everything. And a spear. And the painted arms. He seemed very
out of place and I just kept staring. Then I started figuring how
he might have got here. Maybe Burning Man had a cultural
exchange program. Maybe he was a student at an American university and just put on his traditional garb here on the Playa.
Then I was trying to figure out what to say to him. He was staring back at me and I took a step closer. Then he turned on his
lights—he had battery-powered black lights and fluorescent
paint all over him and he didn't look *anything* like anything
from the Amazon basin.

"Good shit," I thought.

There was a lot of fire there. Out there. Fire spinners. Fire dancers.
Huge churning fire machines like Sherman tanks blasting giant
fireballs into the sky.

*And there's the Erotic Fire Contest where most of the spinners
were dancing naked. One woman had shaved her pubes—safety
first, I suppose.*

The Funk Bus came by. They were playing great music and a
hundred people were dancing along in front of it in the head-

lights, all dressed and synchronized together. It was amazing and we all instantly ran after it.

The Aural Reef

We stepped into the Aural Reef and I lost it. The world changed abruptly and everything was crazy. Totally lollipops-ville. There were huge pieces of driftwood and a giant red fish with white pointy teeth. Sound and distortion were coming from multiple directions, and everything seemed upside down or at weird angles. What had I taken? He didn't tell me it was a double dose. This hadn't happened for years. Whatever reality I had once known was obliterated by the enveloping chaos. It was a beautiful chaos, but like a cartoon or a nightmare. I wasn't sure I could move. Everything was out of scale. Huge jellyfish tentacles were hanging from the ceiling, wherever that was, and stuff was swaying back and forth. I was pressing this big driftwood piece that looked like it was part of a big marimba or some kind of a xylophone. It took a while because of the digital delays and the processor effects but I finally figured out that some of the sound was coming from me and I figured, what the hell, when insane why not enjoy oneself? I played more notes. Someone else was playing some other instrument and somehow we heard each other. I was in Trip City and the year was 29374224, plus or minus an eon or two.

Home. Now I was really home.

The Swimmers

Lolo crawled out of the mouth of the fish and led me by the hand back out onto the Playa. The lasers were cutting giant star swaths across the sky and it seemed like 30,000 freaks had been let loose from their hallucinatory pens. I'd been to the Acid Test but this was beyond by two orders of magnitude. It was "L" night on the Playa.

Somehow we stumbled upon the Swimmers, which was remarkable since I clearly didn't even know what year it was. There was a merry-go-round thing like you find at playgrounds and a circle of full-sized bodies swimming in the dust. If you spun the merry-go-round the swimmers swam harder, but they stayed stuck half in and half out of the surface of the Playa and couldn't get anywhere. A huge strobe light was blinking. The artist had captured Futility. Lolo got it at the same time I did.

We can't help them.

It was the Great Wheel of Samsara.

"How crazy can this get?" I thought. Just then a giant flower came swooping down from the sky.

JF POPE
1998 ©

Scarlett

Scarlett's Pole Dance

Jah told the story:

> *"It was the fourth night of the Pentathalon. We were at Camp*
> *Wow and they were having a pole-dancing contest. Scarlett watched*
> *for a while and said, "I can do that," and got up on the stage and*
> *did it. She was winning too. She was going to get first place when*
> *this woman wearing stilts got up there and completely took over.*
> *Her cunt was right at Scarlett's eye level and she just danced her*
> *off the stage."*

Burning Man

To his immeasurable credit, Larry Harvey has never sold out to corporate interests. He turned down corporate sponsorship and he's kept corporate logos off the Playa. There's plenty of Babylon right in the community. The Burning Man Organization is hoping that its future is in the "regionals"—spin-off festivals—of which there are dozens across the United States and Canada. I've heard them called "franchises" but they're not, at least not in the usual corporate sense. Burning Man gives the regionals philosophy and advice. Sometimes the regionals send back money. It's all very utopian. It sounds too good to be true but it's all evidently quite true. One of the larger regionals is in Seattle.

It's not that no corporate money goes into Burning Man. Some of the big camps are clearly bankrolled—the structures are commercial, not homemade. According to Playa scuttlebutt, Microsoft spent eighty "K" on a camp. It's a rumor. Maybe Microsoft knows whether or not it's true. You can't tell from anything on the Playa. Then there are the stories of high-powered companies sending some of their execs for "team-building" or "creativity-enhancing." Documented, in at least one case.

Kozinets (2002) believes that the temporary nature of the community is an essential part of its success—that being temporary, being built from the Playa each year and taken right back down to the Playa, freezes the community in its formative moment: it is perpetually in the act of creation.

On the Playa

Newbies, first-time Burners, are called virgins. Late, an hour or two before dawn, a very sweet young man had come in and taken his place at the microphone and, after telling us that he was a virgin, added, in a lower voice, "I'm really a virgin." It hadn't been out of his mouth for five seconds when Scarlett seemed to appear from nowhere. I mean, the mic *was* on, but still. She put her hand on his shoulder:

"Do you need any water or anything?"

Our camp Big Sister and Cradle-Robber ...

Maybe it was all coincidence, or all in my imagination. Tripping on the Playa can get so heavy, in a way having nothing to do with the presence or absence of drugs, that knowing what's really going on is, well, not sure where I'm going with this, not sure where I started with this, but it's not all it's cracked up to be, that's for sure. Though it's the "sureness" that gets in the way, actually. I mean, as much as anything is "actual," I mean.

Owl was improvising a rhapsody for Lake Lahontan. "We're in a period of temporary drought," he said, "It'll be back."

Grandfather, I had a dream
Grandfather, tell me what it means.
I saw people, I saw lights
In the waters of Lake Lahontan

Grandfather, I had a dream
Grandfather, tell me what it means.
I saw dust, I saw fire
In the waters of Lake Lahontan

CatGirl came over from Ubercarney. Ubercarney had been blasting psychobilly and surfbilly the whole week. You could hear them at the Man. They were so loud that sometimes we couldn't hear ourselves talk—certainly we couldn't compete musically. It's not that we didn't have the wattage, we did, but we couldn't work around the beat of the canned music. We were trying to sample, to pick up rhythms from the Playa, but the studio sound overpowered everything so we always had to wait until they shut down, around one in the morning, before we could turn on. That's why we were always up until dawn.

Anyway, CatGirl had come over and she was amazed. She said that we were a healing space and she kept bringing young men over from her camp who had bad backs or bad attitudes or suicidal tendencies or something.

On the Playa

Burner girls, dude, Burner girls are the sexiest girls on the planet, period.

To which Regynalonglank replied:

o burner boi, o burner boi i love your sassy kilt
i love your dusty hair and your sunny smile
and your rakish pelvic tilt

On the Playa

Another Ubercarney heavy, Pain Mistress, came over Saturday morning:

"I got dosed last night—who would have thought—just accepting a blue sno cone. Well, I haven't done that kind of thing for a long time. I was in my trailer and really having a hard time when you guys started playing and you just made everything OK."

"That's our medicine," Owl said, "that's what we're really about."

"We didn't know you guys were real people, we thought you were fuckin hippies or something!"

Sigh. We've lost. We should accept it. Maybe all of us, en masse, should just give up and join our blue-collar brothers and sisters in the Republican Party, where at least we'd have a chance to fight it out in the primaries. . . .

I've been trying to be open about my politics here. You don't have to remind me that I'm out of step with America. I have no illusions that my point of view is generally shared on the Playa or that Burning Man is some kind of an upswelling of a new progressive political movement.

Or is it? . . .

Potlatch

Brown recognizes that in the era of HCE ("Here Comes Everybody"), the outcome depends on whether or not the masses settle for vicarious entertainment, Blake's "spectral enjoyment." Spectator. Here, watch the gladiator shed blood, right on your television.

> The Grand Inquisitor is betting that circuses will satisfy.
> The Dionysian bets the Grand Inquisitor is wrong. (Brown
> 1991, pp. 197, 198)

Brown follows Blake, that the violence of Dionysus is preferable to the violence of Mars. That, following Euripides, the suppression of Dionysus leads to the sacrifice of children. And that, following the most ancient threads of religious and magical belief, the rites of Dionysus are prophylactic. Blake wrote: "I will not cease from Mental Fight."

For we have Hirelings in the Camp, the Court, & the University: who would, if they could, for ever depress Mental & prolong Corporeal War.

—Blake, "Milton"

Playing with Fire

Saturday night is the Burn—the burning of the Man. It's hard to stay away from, though some do. All the energy of Black Rock City starts focusing on the middle of the Playa, on the Man. Streams of people start moving toward the Man an hour before the Burn. A large circle is arc'ed out away from the Man, and the rangers keep the massed crowd of 30,000 revelers behind it. Hundreds of fire spinners begin the spectacle. Finally, finally, finally, they set fire to the platform beneath the Man. The Man is packed with hundreds of pounds of fireworks and incendiary powders, and as the flames move up, they start going off. The Man burns with great heat and conflagration, and sometimes wonderful whirlwinds of fire spin out across the Playa, swirling sparks hundreds of feet into the sky and seemingly with a life and volition of their own. It's very exciting. When the Man finally collapses there is a great cheer and the crowd rushes in and dances around the fire as close as they can get without their skin starting to melt.

Some years the mob energy of Burn Night has been too much for me—too much "Burn, baby, burn." One year I had a vision of *Kristallnacht*. It's close to what we do, we can't deny that. It's part of the fire we play with. Spinoza's fire of oneness. Blake's fire of Eternal Delight. The Great Kalpa Fire.

"Burn the fucker!"

Wendell Berry quotes the wisdom of a country neighbor in Kentucky:

"Never let your barn get so messy that only a fire will clean it up."

On the Playa

A big bosomy woman perpetually on the verge of falling out of her Merry Widow corset came in. It was late on Burn Night, when Burners like to talk about the finer points of how it was. She said that she missed the tribal ethos that used to accompany the burn. We agreed that it was kind of a quiet burn.

In 2004 they tried to coordinate the drummers—in the past there would be numerous localized groups, each doing, as it were, their own rhythmic thing. Drummers naturally tend to collect in circles, where they can hear each other. So this year they had central direction, so that all the drummers beat the same beat, and I guess that's what they did and maybe it would have sounded a lot better for the man in the balloon, but it didn't seem to have a lot of fire in it for me and I don't think there was as much dancing.

(I mean, if we formed into ranks and files and practiced and drilled and learned to all kick up our feet at the same time we could probably send an honorary brigade to Nurenberg, Nein?)

The wind started to kick up again, threatening to dust us out of the Adytum. Owl said, "Let's do something about that—Orpheus could. You just have to play something that the wind wants to hear."

The wind blew another gust into the dome, and Owl and Lolo started singing. We found something to play behind them— something that matched the wind that was still kicking up. We finally found a rhythm such that it seemed as if the wind was part of the group, the wind and all of us. Owl started singing softer. None of us could hear what he was singing. We all played softer. A woman sitting in front of us dropped her jaw—she couldn't believe what was happening. We played softer and the wind was quieting with us. When we finally stopped it was dead still.

"It's not like you can just order it," Owl said, "like you're Zeus or someone."

Burning Man

Burning Man represents (my back-of-the-envelope calculation) over a million hours of unpaid volunteer labor. That's a treasure of more than sociological note. The sharks will cruise. The styles and images will be copied by corporate advertising (it's happening already). If co-option fails, attempts at suppression will be redoubled. Titanic temptations will be placed before the Burning Man Organization. Compromise will be presented as a demand, not offered as a choice. The god will either stay or wander on, seeking another breakout of his eternal spring.

It was very late and we weren't sure where we were. On the Playa but wandering, kind of stumbling along hanging on to each other. Suddenly we came upon dinosaur skeletons, one of them mostly buried. Old from before Lake Lahontan ever appeared. Then there was a gallows, with a pterodactyl hanging from it by a chain. As we crept by it, it creaked and moved. But it's not like there was any wind. We moved back and it followed us, staring at us.

This too shall pass.

Inspired Madness

On the Playa

The Temple burns on Sunday. Some camps have already packed up on Sunday, and some are gone entirely, but for many Burners Sunday night is the true climax. David Best's Temples have consistently been constructions of exquisite beauty. Made from the scrap plywood from a large dinosaur-model factory, the Temple is several stories high, a Taj Mahal of intricate arabesques and walls and domes. This year Best and his hundreds of volunteers built wings extending out several hundred feet on either side of the main temple.

The Temple has customarily become a place of remembrance. Thousands of messages and notes and thoughts and testimonials are written or posted on its walls. They are long or short. They are for the absent or the departed, for beloveds or hateds, for lost marriage or new love, lost children or lost friends or for God.

D. D. 2003 RIP

Dad: you were a bastard. You were selfish and uncaring and you hurt us.

John Santos, 1981–2004. I'm here and you live in this burn. Love, Mom.

Lots of stuff gets burned with the Man. I've seen people throw in wedding dresses, hair, dolls, all sorts of stuff—I once burned a book contract—but the Temple burn has a touch of pathos.

I've come to Burning Man to shave my head. The night they burn The Man will be exactly one year to the day since my husband and I separated. I need to mark this anniversary in the true spirit of Burning Man. I need to burn it up. To take this dream of our family, and set fire to it and watch it burn until the ashes blow away. (Fresh, burningman.com)

Crouched beside me, a woman sets up a shrine for her son Chris. Our sons were the same age. . . . (Shannon Kennedy, burningman.com)

On the Playa

We'd ridden out to the Temple early, so that we could sit towards the front. The wait, as every year, seems interminable. We were sitting on the Playa like everyone else. I turned around so we could rest back to back and I got to look at the crowd and talk to our neighbors.

I work 51 weeks a year so I can be here. I took a second job. My father doesn't understand, but he sees how hard I work to get here and he respects that.

A twenty-something young woman. Her friend shared her sentiments. Their camp offered showers, a generous gifting where every drop of water has to be brought in from outside.

When I get out of my car and take my shoes off and put my toes into the Playa dust I know I'm home.

There were shouts of "down in front" and "if you want to stand move to the back" to the few people still standing. One guy, even wearing a huge hat, stubbornly ignored the entreaties of the crowd for ten minutes until it became a chant. Finally the torch was applied. The flames engulfed the structure quickly and it became a huge fire. A giant column of sparks and embers rose hundreds of feet into the sky. Then the wind changed and suddenly the flaming embers were falling all around us.

The crowd leapt to its feet and surged back. Embers were falling everywhere. Someone shouted that they smelled burning hair. Someone rushed by me and said, "Move! Don't just sit there!" I ignored him.

I looked up. It was the most amazing sight I had ever seen. Swirlings and swirlings of embers and fire spinning out of the sky. It was like being in Pompeii. It was entrancing. Embers would land on me and I would brush them off. Big ones and small ones. Some of them mere sparks and some of them burning pieces of charcoal. There were thousands and thousands of them and I was engulfed by the heat of the fire.

Somewhere a gear slipped in my brain and all of a sudden everything was in slow motion and the background of the sky was black, in an absolute sense, like it had been painted black, a full unit blacker than it had been before, whatever units are used for blackness. It was cinematic. And something slipped again and it changed and I was a giant Buddha sitting cross-legged in dust in the Takla Makan or somewhere in Central Asia and there were hundreds of little campfires scattered out for miles around me and then I looked up again and saw the Vortex.

"Where else in the world?" I thought, "Where else wouldn't I be arrested for my own protection, where else wouldn't the powers of insularity have prevented me from experiencing one of the most beautiful spectacles I've ever seen—this event of surpassing beauty."

That's why Burning Man is a miracle. It's a miracle that it exists at all. It's what Hakim Bey calls a "temporary autonomous zone"—a place where the free spirits gather and are able to play for a while, before the Powers of Hegemony learn of their existence and are able to neutralize them. (Bey 1991)

Potlatch

In 1990, the year that Burning Man first moved to the Black Rock Desert, Brown wrote:

> That strengthening of the forces of Eros, for which Freud prayed, might create new institutions of individual generosity and public joy such as the world has not seen since Mont-Saint-Michael and Chartres. . . . Gift-giving, a primary manifestation of Dionysian exuberance, might be able to revel in its own intrinsic self-sacrificial nature, instead of being inhibited and distorted, in bondage to primary social institutions of self-assertion. And public joy might manifest itself in carnivalesque extravaganzas uninhibited by the resentment of the exploited, the excluded, the deprived.

Hope. It gives me hope. That tolerance and self-reliance have a chance in a world that seems headed in the opposite direction. Hope against idolatry, in all of its forms. Hope against bigotry, against all the false consciousness that says it can't be done, against all the false gods of modesty, taste, moderation, and morality. That there can still be, in the twenty-first century, a Feast of Fools, a backwards day of love and heresy, a day for the god named . . . no, let's just call him the god of the potlatch. His alternative worship is war.

Have a great burn.

On the Playa

Monday we finished dismantling the camp. Everybody fanned out searching for MOOP (matter out of place), first in our own camp, and then out on the Playa. Teams of volunteers would be doing the same for many weeks. When Burning Man says "Leave no trace," they mean it. We look for sequins, a loose feather, anything that is not white dust.

And we say goodbyes to our campmates. Like many of the camps, we'll be in touch all the next year, either socially or through email.

Burning Man. Another one!

Yes. Still, for myself, after eight years on the Playa, I think next year I'll go backpacking. Maybe I can find a lake that's still full of water—

uninhibited by the resentment of the exploited, the excluded, the deprived.

Of course, I say that every year.

Coda 2006

In 2006, the weather on the Playa was as good as it gets—mild days, warm nights, only one dust storm. Burning Man continues to change and evolve. Most of the trends outlined in the text continue. There were more kids than ever. The thirty-ish generation are raising families and taking them to the Playa. One five-year-old said, "Burning Man is my favorite place, but it's a little dusty." A four-year-old said, "I know it's past my bedtime, but can I stay up to see the fire dancers?" We'd all been wondering where the fire dancers were, and sure enough, that night they came out.

Second-Generation Burners

I ended up in a camp next to the DPW Ghetto. They were good neighbors. I got to hear "fuck" and "fuckin" used more times in one sentence than I had thought possible. One night they found one of the Belgians from Uchronia passed out on the Playa. After checking his vitals, and finding all well, they stripped him naked and painted him gold.

The Saturday night burn, the burn of the Man, was a slow one. It was a cool burn, a leisurely burn, and the energy gradually moved back across the Playa to the camps, which acted as amplifiers and reflectors. I had to lie down in my tent for awhile. I could hear the booms, shouts, whistles, and rumblings for a mile all around the Playa. When I closed my eyes I could see the energy patterns. The Playa shook and vibrated beneath me. Telepathically, it was all connected.

On Sunday night at the Temple Burn, the entire crowd was silent. Even the art cars and the drunks were quiet. A woman behind me sobbed loudly. A man called out love for his mother. There were tears for lost lovers and friends, or for love that couldn't be. The flames from the towers seemed to toss messages back and forth, lightning-like pulses of red flame shooting up through the smoke far into the sky.

The prayers were accepted.

Several hours later Uchronia burned their huge sculpture at the far side of the Playa, nearly a half-million feet of two-by-threes. The white heat of the conflagration seemed to melt the wood before vaporizing it. This was wasteful consumption in its most naked form. Did I really believe that this could be the alternative to war, or was it madness only?

As the structure collapsed and the fire cooled enough to be approached, people carried stray two-by-threes towards the fire and flung them in. From a distance it looked like a giant procession, a Dionysian army carrying the unfinished crosses of a Christ of Fire. The poles seemed to leap into the flames like salmon jumping at a falls.

On Monday I didn't want to leave. The craziness had become comforting. A packed van going by yelled out thanks to DPW for building Black Rock City. Someone from DPW yelled back "Go the fuck home!"

I sighed and we started breaking camp.

Bibliography

Bey, Hakim. *T.A.Z.: The Temporary Autonomous Zone. Ontological Anarchy, Poetic Terrorism*. Brooklyn: Autonomedia, 1991.

Black, D. S. "Burned by the Man." *SF Life*, Oct. 4, 2000.

Brown, Norman O. *Apocalypse And/Or Metamorphosis*. Berkeley: University of California Press, 1991.

Burning Man. www.burningman.com, 2004.

Burning Man. "What Where When, Vault of Heaven" (festival brochure). 2004.

D'Andrade, Hugh. "Reinventing Politics in Black Rock City." *Burning Man Journal*, Summer-Fall 2004.

Davis, Erik. "Beyond Belief: The Cults of Burning Man," in Gilmore and Van Proyen, 2005. Originally distributed as a privately printed brochure: "BRC."

Davis, Erik. *Techgnosis: Myth, Magic + Mysticism in the Age of Information*. New York: Three Rivers Press, 1998.

Doherty, Brian. *This Is Burning Man: The Rise of a New American Underground*. New York: Little, Brown & Co., 2004.

ePlaya, www.eplaya.burningman.com, 2004.

Ehrenreich, Barbara. *Blood Rites: Origins and History of the Passions of War*. New York: Metropolitan, 1997.

Ehrenreich, Barbara. "Transcendence, Hope & Ecstasy." *Z Magazine*, October 1998.

Falassi, Alessandro, ed. *Time Out of Time: Essays on the Festival*. Albuquerque: University of New Mexico Press, 1987.

Frank, Thomas. *What's the Matter with Kansas? How Conservatives Won the Heart of America.* New York: Metropolitan Books, 2004.

Fresh. "Burn It," in "Tales from the Playa," www.burningman.com, 2004.

Gilmore, Lee, and Mark Van Proyen, eds. *AfterBurn: Reflections on Burning Man.* Albuquerque: University of New Mexico Press, 2005.

Harvey, Larry. Playa Speech, www.burningman.com/whatisburningman, 1997.

Higgins, Hannah. *Fluxus Experience.* Berkeley: University of California Press, 2002.

Itzkoff, Dave. "The Rite of Summer." *New York Times,* Sept. 19, 2004.

Kennedy, Shannon. "Green Monkey," in "Tales from the Playa," www.burningman.com, 2004.

Kozinets, Robert. "Can Consumers Escape the Market? Emancipatory Illuminations from Burning Man," *Journal of Consumer Research, Inc.,* Vol. 29, June 2002.

Kreuter, Holly. *Drama in the Desert: The Sights and Sounds of Burning Man.* San Francisco: Raised Barn Press, 2002.

Lebel, Jean-Jacques. Interview with Saul Gottlieb in *Boss #2,* edited by Reginald Gay. 1967.

Pendell, Dale. *Pharmako Gnosis: Plant Teachers and the Poison Path.* San Francisco: Mercury House, 2006.

Pinchbeck, Daniel. "Heat of the Moment: The Art and Culture of Burning Man." *ArtForum,* Nov. 2003.

Piss Clear. Edited by Adrian Roberts. 8:00, Orion's Belt & Venus, Black Rock City, 2004.

Riesel, René, and Alain Leauthier. Translated by Tom McDonough. "Submission is Advancing at a Frightful Speed." Interview in *Liberation*, www.situationist.cjb.net, Situationist International Online, 2001.

Sandford, Mariellen R., ed. *Happenings and Other Acts*. New York: Routledge, 1995.

Streng, George. www.imageevent.com/photogenics/burningman, 2003.

Traub, Barbara, John Plunkett, and Janelle Brown, eds. *Burning Man*. Hardwired, 1997.

Wray, Matt. "Burning Man and the Rituals of Capitalism," *Bad Subjects*, Issue # 21, 1995 (quoted in Kozinets).

About the Author

Dale Pendell is the author of the acclaimed *Pharmako* trilogy, an encyclopedic (and eccentric) study of psychoactive plants. His poetry is widely anthologized; he was the founding editor of the avant-garde magazine *Kuksu*, and a co-founder of the Primitive Arts Institute. He has worked as a botanist, a carpenter, a mechanic, and a computer scientist for companies such as Imagen, Phoenix Technologies, and Adobe Systems. "Poets have license," Dale says. He continues to attend Burning Man, under new identities.

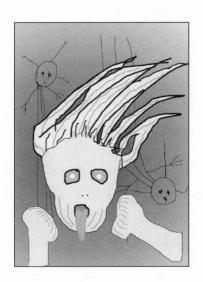

About the Artist

Just Freeman Pope (1936–2000) was born in Sacramento and raised in Watsonville, California. He received AB and MA degrees in experimental psychology from the University of California, Berkeley, and went on to study art under the tutelage of Wayne Thiebaud and other artists such as George Herms. He had shows of his engravings, ivory and bone work, and metal jewelry at the De Young Museum, the Oakland Museum, and many other galleries. He was also a jazz pianist and composer, and worked with the Open Theatre in Berkeley. He worked variously at a foundry in Berkeley, at the Stanford Linear Accelerator, and as a partner in a natural foods store in Davis. He also dabbled in computer programming, mostly in eight-bit assembly code for long-vanished machines.

Just suffered a severe stroke in the early 1980s that left him paralyzed and speechless. Over the next decade and a half, through extraordinary effort, he regained the use of the left half of his body, eventually being able to walk with a cane and to drive. Somehow he also relearned to speak, using a sometimes-limited vocabulary in delightfully creative and slurry ways. He married Mira Talbott, of Chico, in the early 1990s, and spent his last years designing and creating computer art, bronze castings, and jewelry. He never made it to Burning Man. He would have felt very much "at home."